1 MONTH OF FREE READING

at
www.ForgottenBooks.com

By purchasing this book you are eligible for one month membership to ForgottenBooks.com, giving you unlimited access to our entire collection of over 700,000 titles via our web site and mobile apps.

To claim your free month visit:

www.forgottenbooks.com/free169552

* Offer is valid for 45 days from date of purchase. Terms and conditions apply.

ISBN 978-0-266-17545-2
PIBN 10169552

This book is a reproduction of an important historical work. Forgotten Books uses state-of-the-art technology to digitally reconstruct the work, preserving the original format whilst repairing imperfections present in the aged copy. In rare cases, an imperfection in the original, such as a blemish or missing page, may be replicated in our edition. We do, however, repair the vast majority of imperfections successfully; any imperfections that remain are intentionally left to preserve the state of such historical works.

Forgotten Books is a registered trademark of FB &c Ltd.
Copyright © 2017 FB &c Ltd.
FB &c Ltd, Dalton House, 60 Windsor Avenue, London, SW19 2RR.
Company number 08720141. Registered in England and Wales.

For support please visit www.forgottenbooks.com

BOOK OF VERSES.

AUGUSTUS MENDON LORD.

CAMBRIDGE:
1886.

COPYRIGHT, 1886,
BY AUGUSTUS MENDON LORD.

PRIVATELY PRINTED.

*David Clapp & Son, Printers,
35 Bedford St., Boston.*

CONTENTS.

	Page.
Boating	11
Eastern Windows	14
The Song of the Saybrook Meadows .	15
Courage	17
Soft o'er the Hills of Lancaster . .	19
Aurea Mediocritas	20
The Dark Day	21
Strength	22
O Bonnie Hills of Leicester . . .	23
Compromise	24
Winnipesaukee	26
Longfellow's Portrait	28
Hampton Beach	29
Example	30
Oh for the Storm-Scarred Headlands .	31
On the Fly-Leaf of Froissart's Chronicles	33
Major and Minor	34

CONTENTS.

A Breath of Fresh Air	35
Oak Cliff	36
I said "I Will be Wise"	38
Mari Magno	42
Learning Hath Knights	43
North Conway	44
A New Year's Prayer	46
Bald Head Cliff	47
Straight On	49
Mother	50
Vacation Friends	52
Free Lances	53
Farewell to the Hills	54
Hugh Cressy,—Benedictine	57

TO MY MOTHER.

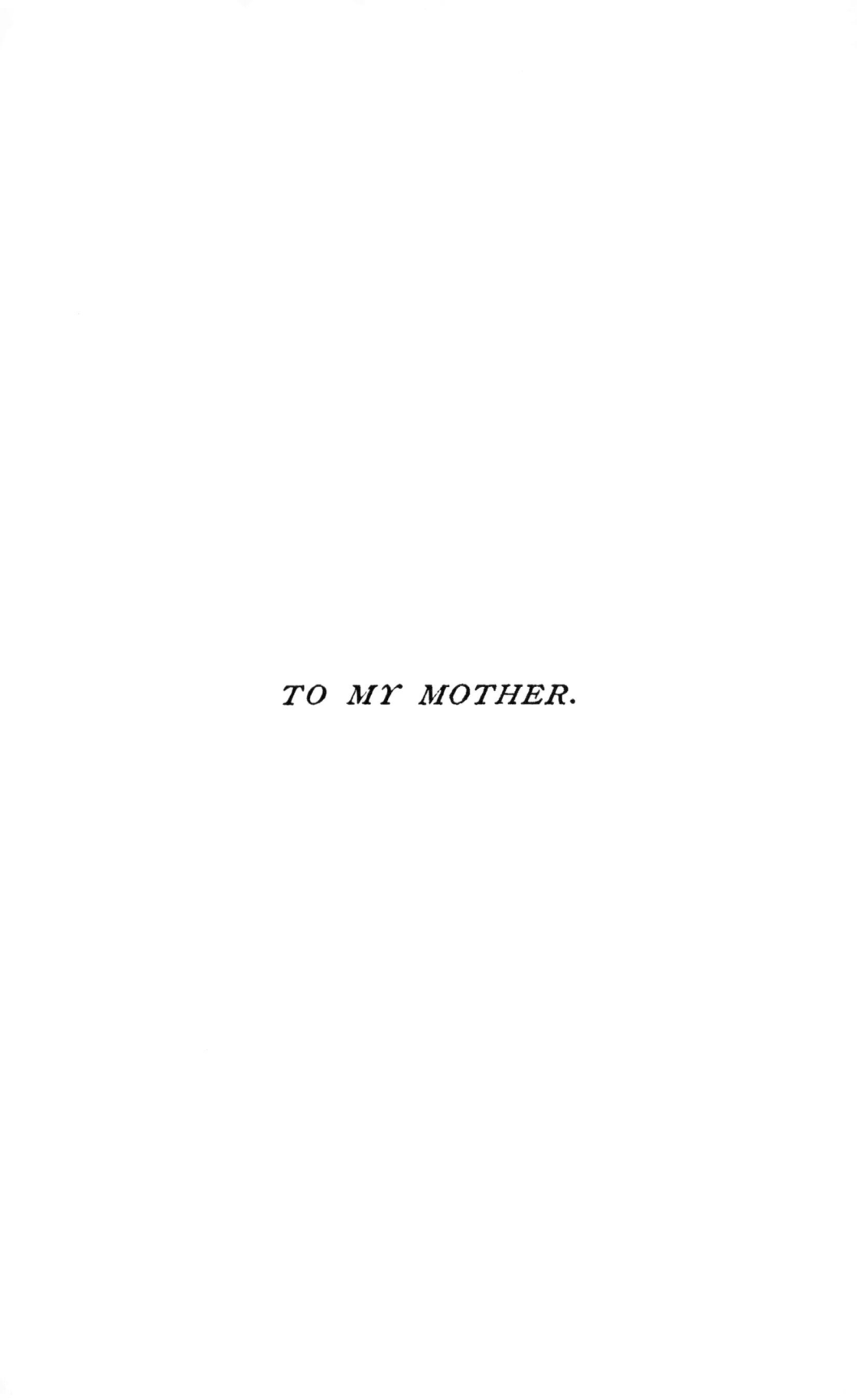

A BOOK OF VERSES.

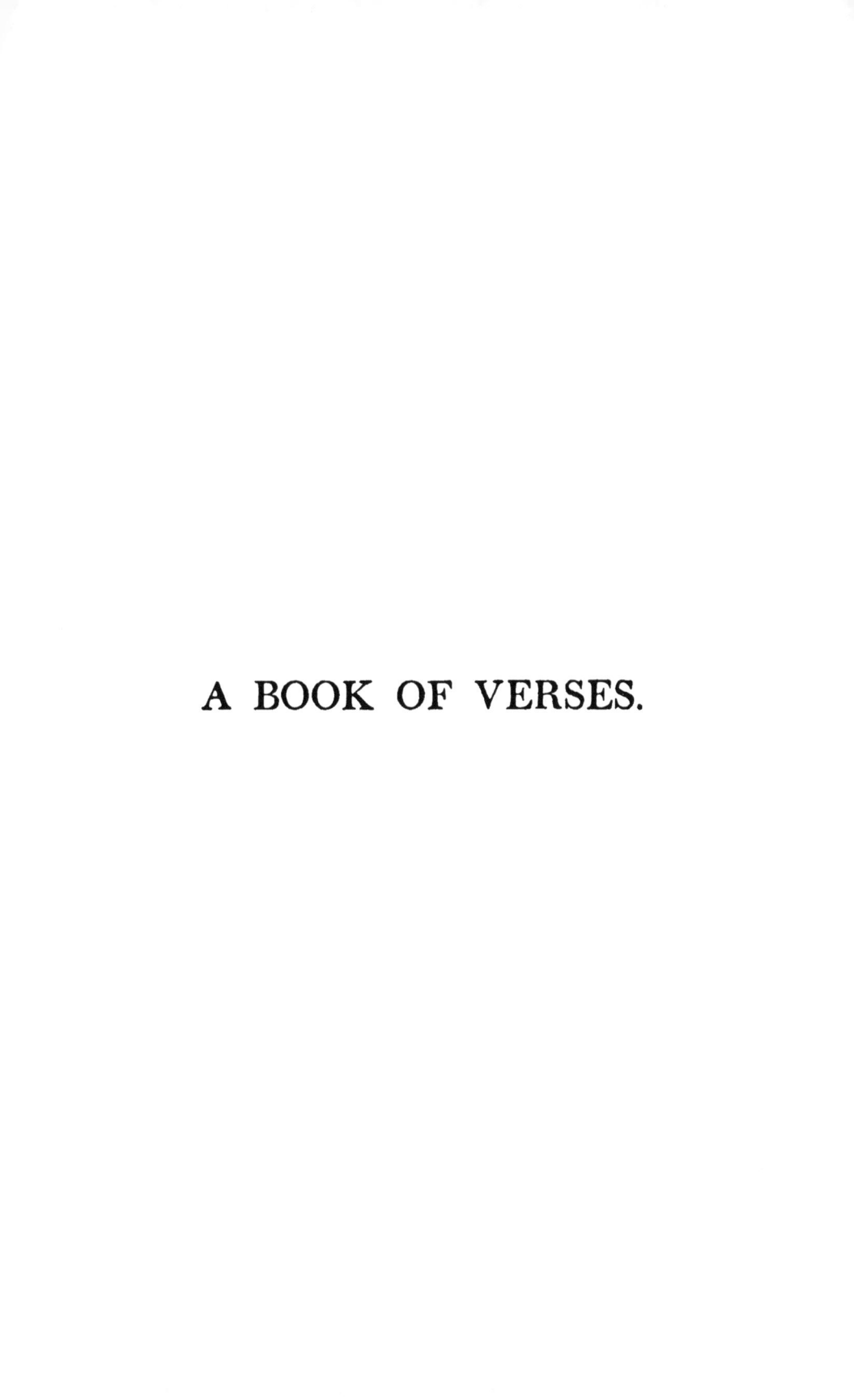

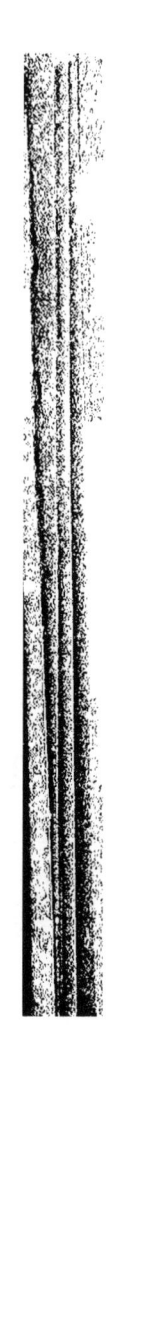

BOATING.

A JUNE day, cool from recent rain;
The sky without a speck or stain
To mark the gray storm's toil and stress;
The brimming river rippleless.
Into the stream the long boat swings;
Soft drop her oars, like sinewy wings,
And more than lifeless steel and wood,
She leaps into the middle flood.
Her strength is ours, our will is hers,
One life within us thrills and stirs.
What joy with rhythmic sweep and sway
To fly along the liquid way,
To feel each tense-drawn muscle strain,
And hear the dripping blade's refrain;
Or, resting on the level oar,
To drift beside the dusky shore
Through green pads whispering as we pass,
And bending beds of pickerel grass,

And watch with eager, grateful eye
The woodland's changing pageantry:
The gnarled oaks spreading broad and low,
The elms that like leaf-fountains grow;
Ash, chestnut, lightsome maple grove,
With elder-thickets interwove,
And sharply clear against the green
The swaying birch's silver sheen.
We catch the smell of sun-warmed pines,
Of marsh-pinks, and of wild-grape vines,
And scent, to make the bee's heart glad,
Of pungent Balm of Gilead.
And now, in sunlight once again,
We round the headland's narrow plain;
Three strokes, and on the shelving sand
We bring the willing boat to land;
Then off through stubbly pasture dells
Sparse-set with cedar sentinels,
To where in cool, leaf-laughing nook
Slips o'er the stones the swollen brook.
Outstretched full length beside the stream,
We lie half waking, half in dream,
And feast our ears with woodland notes.
Down the warm air the wren's song floats,

BOATING.

Sharp trumpets out the angry jay;
Hark! from some tree-top far away
The cat-bird's saucy answer falls;
And, when all else is silent, calls,
Deep bowered on some shady hill,
The day-caught, sleepy whip-poor-will.
But look! the level sunbeams shine
Along the tree trunks' gleaming line;
A sea of gold, the water fills
The purple circle of the hills.
Home then our sparkling path we trace,
The sunset's glory in our face,
Which fades and fades, till as we reach
The low pier and the shingly beach,
On stream, and wood, and hill-top bare
The moon's soft light lies everywhere.

Charles River, Waltham, Mass.

EASTERN WINDOWS.

WE sat beside the casement high
   That opened on the eastern sea;
Thy thoughts were on the star-lit sky,
   But mine were still on thee.

And as I watched thy fine, brave face,
   I wished my heart were more like thine —
As full of hope and tender grace,
   As full of light divine.

Thy windows ope on eastern skies,
   Undimmed by sadness or regret;
Thou see'st fair stars and planets rise,
   But never see'st them set.

THE SONG OF THE SAYBROOK MEADOWS.

Ah, youth is like a summer night,
 Too soon must come the morrow;
Its stainless missal of delight
 Too soon be closed by sorrow!

The golden moon shone softly down
 Across the Saybrook meadows,
And filled their breezy leagues of brown
 With misty lights and shadows.

And far away long, trembling gleams
 Above the dark dunes lifted,
Showed where beneath its steady beams
 The smooth sea glanced and shifted.

With many a tale and glad refrain
 Our lingering way we wended;
But ever with our gayest strain
 The sea's low murmur blended.

And ever o'er our careless glee
    There came a hush unbidden;
A voice spoke from the rocking sea
    Words in our own hearts hidden: —

Ah, youth is like a summer night,
    Too soon must come the morrow;
Its stainless missal of delight
    Too soon be closed by sorrow!

COURAGE.

You tell me that life is not what I dream,
   That man is selfish and woman vain;
That the strong are made strong through suffering,
   And the wise are wise but in bearing pain;
That our souls are filled with earthly dust,
   The glory fades from our skies away,
And the human heart, like the mountain pine,
   Sings a song of grief on the brightest day.

Yet must we live for petty aims,
   And say perfection exists nowhere?
I see but house-plants — well, what then?
   The fields are green and the hills are fair.
Better good dreams than evil facts,
   A noble faith than ignoble deeds.
My path may not run through fruits and flowers,
   Must I therefore fill my hands with weeds?

I know, I know they must die away,
   The altar-lights of the misty dawn;
We worship no more at the shrines of youth,
   Their idols are broken, their splendor gone.
Yet, hoping on as best we may,
   Whatever makes, or whatever mars,
It can be no crime, if our feet grow tired,
   Though the dust be nearest, to look at the stars.

Not on life's doubters life's glories fall;
   The bridegroom comes, but they go not in.
Who lives for bread shall eat but bread,
   And what we strive for that we win.
We must labor on till the long day's close;
   We shall know life's meaning then. Ah, well,
We may find it true in the end — who knows? —
   The old tale of the angel and Israel.

SOFT O'ER THE HILLS OF LANCASTER.

SOFT o'er the hills of Lancaster
   The Autumn evening fell,
When last you pressed my lingering hand,
   And, laughing, said farewell.

I heard your deep, young, earnest voice
   Familiar fall and rise,
And saw at times your purpose strong
   Light up your clear brown eyes.

The sunset fades o'er Lancaster,
   The dear old hills grow dim,
And as of old the harvest moon
   Hangs o'er Wachusett's rim.

But you to-night are far away
   Beside a foreign sea,
And the moon-lit hills of Lancaster
   Are fair, but not to me.

AUREA MEDIOCRITAS.

To fawn and pander to our own conceit,
   In guise of search for truth or love of beauty,
To warp the soul's growth in the wasteful heat
   Of passion for some vague ideal duty, —
Is this life's best aim? — nay, then, yield the prize
   To short-lived pains, and joys that cannot bless,
And blind the spirit's upward-looking eyes
   With petty dust of little meannesses!
In God's world we must live, and not in one
Made up of our own dreams and whims, nor shun
   Its hopes and doubts, its erring love and hate.
"Yes," said a voice, "thy anger is half just;
Yet in that higher vision keep thy trust;
   Work in the small, inspired by the great!"

THE DARK DAY.

A LOW gray sky, a freshening wind,
    A cold scent of the misty sea;
Before, the barren dunes; behind,
    The level meadows far and free.

And hark! from o'er the bleak sea-wall
    A muffled intermittent roar;
The swinging surf's slow rise and fall
    Around the desolate kelp-strewn shore.

STRENGTH.

Oh, make me wise to see the things that are!
   The gods have filled the earth with blinding show;
A trembling leaf may hide a distant star,
   The clear moon pales before a watch-fire's glow.

Oh, make me brave! lest when my eyes have seen,
   My soul in vain with love or fear may strive;
The bow is bent, the arrow straight and keen,
   Let fly! though through thy kinsman's heart it drive.
Oh, make me strong! lest when I fain would speak,
   My lips may fail to tell the truth I meant;
Strength need I most, for if the soul be weak,
   Courage is pain, and wisdom discontent.

O BONNIE HILLS OF LEICESTER.

O BONNIE hills of Leicester, full many years are run
Since o'er your downs I wandered in shadow and in sun.
The breezy mountain pastures, the cool, bird-haunted woods,
The old, elm-shadowed homesteads, where deepest quiet broods —
All, all unchanged, as if a boy I'd dreamed an hour away,
And waked to find the same green woods, the same sweet summer day.

O bonnie hearts of Leicester, whose warmth my childhood knew,
Though eyes may dim and cheeks may fade, will you not beat as true?
I dream the glad days over, my boyhood's bright romance,
I meet your eyes and press your hands, I join in song and dance.
Ah! years may come and years may go, and if they bring but ill,
O bonnie hearts of Leicester will live in memory still.

COMPROMISE.

"The state is out of joint!" ah, think not then,
Ideal good to force on erring men.
This is the rock where all your visions break, —
What is the best the people choose to take?

Our nature's double, favor neither half,
Hamlet admire, and yet at Falstaff laugh,
Pure end, pure motive, — 'tis an idle tale;
Be virtuous, — but disdain not "cakes and ale."

O hapless truth! and yet if truth indeed,
How vain to turn, or shrink, or weakly plead;
Farewell, great faith unwitting youth that blessed;
Hail, tainted wit and shrewd-tongued interest.

Oh, I had thought that what we dearest prize,
Had nobler origins than compromise;
Had thought that Salamis and Lexington
By men of iron will were fought and won.

Columbus, Cromwell, Luther, Socrates, —
No cowed, obsequious sycophants were these;
Their hearts lit up with more than human fire,
They caught the courage of their high desire.

Yes, even in these doubtful latter days,
When night seems near, and dark grow all the ways,
May we not still that purer life profess,
Which once we taste, all else is bitterness?

And shall we juggle with those loftier laws
For sneering worldlings' selfish, half-applause,
Who, in the end, our serving all forgot,
Would spew us out as neither cold nor hot!

WINNIPESAUKEE.

On the steep headland plumed with lofty pines,
   Stretched in the shadowed silence soft and brown,
I lie and watch the long, blue slanting lines
   Of scented sunshine slowly loiter down
Through close-wove glooms of verdure; far above,
The slender, tufted tops scarce seem to move
   Against the sunlit sky's deep monotone.

And far below, clear, rippleless, serene,
   On either side the waters stretch away
To where the cloud-swept hills stand, massed in green,
   Guarding the azure gates of night and day.

Oh, this is life! only to lie and dream,
   To feel the sunshine creep into the blood
And warm the heart, like healing balm; to seem
   A part of all we see, — earth, air and flood, —
While thoughts, unfettered, pass unheeded by
   As the wild flowers plucked, and then, in careless mood,
Dropped from the loosened hand, forgotten lie.

Lo! while I dream, the golden-lippèd sun
  Kisses the blushing waters, slowly fills
The trembling lake with glory, and is gone, —
  Fled like a smile across the darkening hills.

Farewell, dear Day! thine influence is one
  That melts into our being; thou shalt go
Into the crowded streets with us, and tone
  Our intercourse with man with thine own glow
Of tenderness; and in the lonely hour
Stir hidden soul-depths with mysterious power,
  And flood the eye with sudden overflow.

LONGFELLOW'S PORTRAIT.

AH! sweet the cadence of immortal lines,
    The songs men love to sing;
But sweeter yet the soul that through them shines,
    The life from which they spring, —

The soul youth's passion, manhood's selfishness
    Warped not, nor stained with wrong,
And Age's winter folds in its caress
    Still unsubdued and strong.

Yet in its strength not arrogant or cold,
    But broad in sympathies, —
A man symmetrical! such dreamed of old
    Plato and Socrates!

Yes, well we crown him with song's highest meed,
    His words immortal call, —
But they who see that calm, grand face, may read
    The noblest song of all!

February 27, 1882.

HAMPTON BEACH.

Down the white road, slow-winding to the sea,
   Through sunny inland farms, where sleeping lie
   Shadow-swept fields of corn and golden rye,
Or where the summer wind mysteriously
Chants to the pines its sea-born melody;
   Or where, from plains of stubble, brown and dry,
   The lofty elms stand clear against the sky,
I loiter on, with careless step and free.
I hear the distant ocean breathing low,
   Like some vast Titan wrapped in easy sleep;
Fanned by the strong wings of the freshening breeze,
I feel new life through all my being flow,
   The unworn healing of the mighty deep,
The solemn benediction of the seas.

EXAMPLE.

Thou canst not others' fetters break
   While thou remain'st a slave;
The thoughtless others thoughtless make,
   The brave make others brave.

And even the weakest in the fight
   Wear valor's noblest charm,
Who pray, not for a sword more light,
   But for a stronger arm.

OH FOR THE STORM-SCARRED HEAD-LANDS.

OH for the storm-scarred headlands,
    The hoarse, unresting seas;
The shifting mist and sunshine,
    The cool, salt eastern breeze!

Oh to trace the low pine woodlands,
    Or walk the windy shore,
Or feel the muscle tighten
    Against the straining oar!

Sweeter than harp or sackbut
    To weary ear and brain,
The lapwing's low, wild whistle,
    The sea-gull's angry skane.

Better than books or study
    On gorse-grown cliffs to lie,
And watch the cloud-wrack slowly
    Climb up the summer sky.

Oh for the blackened headlands,
The hoarse, tumultuous seas,
The trailing mists and shadows,
The strong, salt eastern breeze!

ON THE FLY LEAF OF FROISSART'S CHRONICLES.

To M. G.

THOUGH idle now hang sword and lance,
   We need the knightly virtues still;
Persistence, courage, temperance,
   Unblemished honor, iron will.

These stirring tales of chivalry,
   Accept them for my friendship's sake;
Not vainly given, if in thee
   A kindred nature they awake;

And lead thee on, with simple art,
   A noble life to wisely plan,
That thou may'st bear a knightly heart,
   And be a worthy gentleman.

MAJOR AND MINOR.

Clear shines the sun, fresh blows the mountain wind,
And as I pass I give one look behind:
The red-roofed town, the gray church on the hill,
The river winding through the meadows still, —
Sweet is the scene, — 'twill linger for a day,
But earth is ample and my heart is gay;
Far o'er the dim blue mountains I must go,
To seek a larger life than here I know;
Farewell, farewell, my path lies far away
From home and friends and bonnie Mailleraie.

* * * * * * * * *

The sky is dark, and spectre-like the rain
Sweeps from the hills and hides the distant plain;
The dark pines murmur as the wind grows strong,
My feet are weary and the way is long;
Oh for the house that poplars tall surround,
The garden and the low hills vineyard-crowned,
Only to walk the sunny banks of Seine,
And meet the dear old faces once again,
Only to see, before they fade for aye,
Home and the deep blue skies of Mailleraie.

A BREATH OF FRESH AIR.

So from the crowded rooms, from the giggling and dancing and singing,
(Singing Italian of course, and dancing one long weary waltz),
Into the cool spring night he passed with a deep breath of freedom;
Broad on his eager sight broke the blue reaches of sky,
And from the budding trees and the newly-turned loam of the farm lands,
Fresh to his nostrils, came the scents of revivified growth.
Grateful the stillness was, unbroken save by the piping,
Rhythmic and softly clear, of frogs in the river beyond;
Only on crossing the bridge, when he stopped to listen more closely,
This, too, suddenly ceased—dead silence in water and air;
But as he turned away and left the river behind him,
Lo! the soft piping began, rhythmic and clear as before.

OAK CLIFF.

Up from the dusty village street,
Through the gate o'er which the dark oaks meet,
  Thick grown with mosses and trailing vines,
    I enter the dear old place once more.
Calm and clear in the noontide still
Stand garden and orchard and wood-crowned hill,
  And guarded by two great broad-boughed pines,
    The sunny house with its open door,
Fair in itself, and yet more fair
That the grace of memory lingers there.
  Ah! the long, bright days in the deep-pathed woods
    And the meadows' sunny solitudes;
And the summer nights when the master's hand
  Charmed from the clavichord's silent keys
  Sweet half-forgotten old melodies, —
  Who has not known them? — that bring the pain
  And the joy of lost boyhood back again,
And wide-eyed childhood's fairyland.
  Dear old scenes, I know at last
  Life's greatest mystery is the past.

The subtle grace of those days is fled;
   That the fruit may grow, the blossoms fall.
   Yet the heart cannot think that this is all;
The spirit sleepeth, but is not dead.
Somewhere in God's hidden destinies
   The child's fresh heart and the man's large mind
   Will meet and mingle, and we shall find
The secret of life's lost harmonies.

West Medford, Mass.

I SAID "I WILL BE WISE."

"I said, 'I will be wise,' but it was far from me."
The words come back as purposeless I lie
Here where the strong, warm wind goes rushing by,—
        An unseen sea,
That bends and sways the larches high,
And breaks in undiminished flow
With murmuring roar among the oaks below.

Wisdom, did I not seek thee once, what time,
        Night after night
        The winter fields lay white
In awful stillness 'neath the deep, cold skies?
Did I not share the golden reveries
Of Plato, read with joyful eyes
The Tuscan poet's beautiful old rhyme,
        Or trace the wild,

I SAID "I WILL BE WISE."

Majestic fantasies of Avon's matchless child,
Until my heart grew hot with vain desire
      To catch thy sacred fire,
And looking out with vision calm and clear,
To speak one word the world might pause to hear!

      Alas! alas! the word
Trembled upon my lips, but it was never heard;
The hand just raised dropped nerveless to my side,
      And treacherous I denied
(Poor, coward soul), my sworn allegiance.
      Woe's me! what luckless chance
Brought that loose roisterer, Pleasure, to my door,
      Who all night long
      With roaring jest and song
Scoffed at the quiet sweetness of thy lore?

And I — I yielded till, the night nigh spent,
Secretly sneering at my fall, she went.
      Bowed down with shame,
I dared not even whisper thy dear name;
Dared not return to feel with keen disgrace
The stern, sad look on thy reproving face;
But knowing thy fair gifts were forfeited,
Followed where'er that baser service led.

Yet now that genial summer time is here,
        When Nature, fain to make redress
        For rude ungraciousness,
Through all the fickle weeks of Spring severe,
Flings wide her treasures in the long sweet days,
And floods with bloom these lightsome hillside ways,
May I not hope that thou too wilt relent,
And with thine olden pity haste to meet
        My long-estrangèd feet?
Oh, say not 'tis too late that I repent!

I hear the robin busy in the cherry tree,
The saucy blue-bird jodling out his glee,
        And, faint and far,
The village clock's slow stroke familiar;
I claim as friends the flowers that nod their heads
In the old-fashioned, sunny garden beds;
Each shady slope, each pebbly, winding path
        A wondrous power hath
With chiding memories to fill the heart.

Oh, let that former nearness plead
        The greatness of my need,
And take me back; I will no more depart!

I ask not now to stand
Among thy chosen band,
The poets and the prophets; only grant me grace
To be thy servant in the lowliest place.
Yea, even there, O Wisdom, thou may'st bless
With joys that cannot cease;
For "all thy ways are ways of pleasantness,
And all thy paths are peace!"

MARI MAGNO.

On smoother tide the summer moon ne'er shone,
   The steady reef-lights burn far out at sea;
The boat grates on the sand and then is gone;
   " Farewell, farewell, the night so short will be
And with the dawn I shall return to thee!"
   "Return, return to thee!" echoes the smiling sea.

The morning whitens over wave and sand,
   The mist lifts up and hastens out to sea,
And others' lovers long have come to land;
   But my own love returns no more to me.
"Returns no more, returns no more to me!"
   Echoes the smiling sea, the careless, mocking sea.

LEARNING HATH KNIGHTS.

Learning hath knights of purpose strong,
    Unselfish, but unpitying,
Careless — so they but crush their wrong, —
    Of other wrong they cause to spring.

Their life, nor love. nor grief, alloys,
    Their heart ne'er tasted youth's romance;
They scorn our little, needed joys,
    As Michal mocked at David's dance.

But Learning's kings (thy dream is good)
    Are gentle; power is their's through pain.
Sharers in pleasure's loftiest mood,
    They know her humblest is not vain;

And, loving truth, feel greater need
    Than books alone can satisfy;
As Arabs, when Koran they read,
    Leave their tents open to the sky.

NORTH CONWAY.

To P. C.

FAIR was the scene—I see it even now, —
   Forest and farm, and winding stream that fills
Conway's elmed fields with beauty, and beyond
   The soft uprising of the wooded hills.
Oh, beautiful! and yet more beautiful
   That noble soul who walked these fields with me,—
   A voice, a touch, a heart, that seemed to be
The higher portion of the perfect whole.

How often in the shadow of the pines
   We sat together dreaming dreams of good,
Or walked the breezy meadows, or beside
   The woodgirt stillness of the Saco's flood.
Oh, then were holy thoughts and holier dreams,
   Half-spoken hopes, upliftings unto prayer,
   Outlooks toward life with prospects broad and fair,
And deep discussion of beloved themes.

NORTH CONWAY.

The ever-changing glory of the hills,
   The sunny meadow, and the gloomy wood,
Silver-voiced brook and mountain-circled lake,
   And calm, clear deeps of blue that overbrood,
Flushed with the rising or the setting sun, —
   All with that lofty spirit seemed to blend.
   O fair, sweet scene! O noble-hearted friend!
Memory looks back, and lo! ye are as one.

A NEW YEAR'S PRAYER.

Oh, calm and sweet this winter day
  Of pure white earth and cloudless sky!
Life's cares, like cloud-wreaths, fade away;
  In God's own hand I seem to lie.
Good books, dear friends, and scenes so fair, —
Ah, they can make each day a prayer,
  Each night a benedicite.

O Thou, to whom my glad soul turns,
  Unburdened yet by toil and stress,
The light that in my spirit burns
  Let me not waste in selfishness!
Teach me to strive a manly strife,
And let me live an earnest life,
  Some truth reveal, some wrong redress.

Oh, keep me true to that high dream
  That smote my upward looking face!
Let me not sink my life's fresh stream
  In dull, cold sands of commonplace.
So shall the evening air be bright,
So shall the self-same glory light
  My western, as my eastern, skies.

BALD HEAD CLIFF.

The dark rock lifts its monolith gigantic
  In mighty stairs clear cut against the sky,
And sudden falls to where the cold Atlantic
  Welters and whitens ineffectually.

First a long hush as if the smooth waves scheming
  Whispered some secret watchword down their line,
Then in close ranks with wild foam banners streaming
  They dash clear up the boulders' black incline;

In vain, the upper wall with front reliant
  Unyielding meets their onset's crushing roar,
And the green waters routed, but defiant,
  In maddened circles backward crowd and pour.

Hour after hour I watch them falling, lifting,
  And hear the crisp splash of the whirling spray;
Or turn to see the half lights strangely shifting
  Along the cliff's far heights and hollows gray;

The storm-stained heights where loving eyes discover
  Soft mingled colors delicately laid,
And tufts of furze where white-winged sea-birds hover,
  Flashing across the purple depths of shade.

So mid the surf's hoarse roar and strife, impassive
  The great crag stands in awful loneliness,
While gently round its peaks and ledges massive
  The lingering summer folds its last caress.

York, Maine.

STRAIGHT ON.

METHOUGHT I saw a pilgrim journeying slow
  Along a dusty road. On either side
  Lay wood, and field, and meadow spreading wide
With wind-swept rows of blossom all aglow.
Kingly his bearing and his face, although
  Scarred with past pain, broad browed and noble-eyed.
And thus he spake: "Here would I fain abide,
And walk in peace the pleasant fields below;
Yet must I move straight on, for though my soul
  See not the distant Canaan I shall tread,
    Clear as of old from youth's high mountains, still,
  That end once seen, all lower good is ill.
  Yea, onward straight, in all ways limited,
Except in the direction of my goal."

MOTHER.

Year by year I move away
From the morning of my day,
Boyhood's work and boyhood's play
But a dream within a dream.

I have walked the world of men,
Wearied hands and worried brain,
Learned and unlearned, learned again,
Broken many a cherished scheme.

Still "I would" yields to "I ought;"
All the shrewd-eyed world has taught
Is but ashes and as naught
To the lessons learned of thee.

Fades the poet's light and bloom,
Sage's wisdom turns to gloom;
Oh, the twilight darkened room,
And the talks beside thy knee!

MOTHER.

Friends are mine well-tried and true,
Heart and head we loved and grew;
But we have our tasks to do,
Tasks we may not reconcile.

And I feel that one alone
Lives a life within my own;
Praise or blame upon me thrown
Fades before a mother's smile.

VACATION FRIENDS.

Soft fell the quiet evening's grateful gloom,
   The old clock ticked its warning clear and slow,
   And strangely with the firelight's fitful glow
The moonlight mingled in the silent room,
All silent, save the far-off murmuring boom
   Of seas that Autumn urged to higher flow,
   And from the sere, brown stubble-fields below
The crickets shrilly piping Summer's doom.
We sat and spoke not, friends whom chance had brought
   Together from the city's toil and roar,
   Companions of bright days by sea and field;
Yet in that brief hour of unuttered thought
   We felt, I knew, of truest friendship more
   Than all the merry summer had revealed.

Dow Cottage, Hampton, N. H.

FREE LANCES.

A-RIDING, a-riding, i'the growing morning light!
The bugles blow, and all a-row our lances glitter bright.
Along the winding river, beside the beachèd sea,
By lonely tower, or high-walled town, or heathy wastes of lea;
Where'er we go, whate'er good cause our strong right arms may claim,
God guide us, merry gentlemen, and keep our swords from shame!

We cater for no lady's whims, we serve nor church nor lords,
But worship upon God's green hills and love our own bright swords.
Let friars pray, and striplings love, and courtiers bend the knee,
While blood is hot and muscle firm, our hearts and hands are free.
A-riding a-riding, — the east is all a-flame!
God guide us, merry gentlemen, and keep our swords from shame.

FAREWELL TO THE HILLS!

"Goodbye sweet days, goodbye, goodbye!" the song
Floated across the mellow autumn air,
And echoed faintly from the purple hills,
And fainter still within me woke a voice
Reluctant answering "goodbye, goodbye!"
Goodbye still mornings when the level mist
Spread a white shroud across the valley lands,
And made the craggy mountain peaks appear
As rocky islands in a shoreless sea;
Till with the sun upsprang a freshening wind
That tossed the troubled vapor to and fro
And rolled it back against the mountain walls,
And blew it off into the deepening sky.

Goodbye long climbs through winding forest paths,
With broad-boughed fir and cedar redolent,
Where searching sunlight fell in flaky gleams
On quivering leaves and beds of velvet moss,
Or opened fairy vistas suddenly

FAREWELL TO THE HILLS.

Into the gloomy wood. And when at last
The goal was reached, what joy unutterable!
From off our rocky pinnacle the woods
Fell in great folds, as of some royal robe,
Sweeping far out into the rolling plain
To meet the threadlike river, — whence again
New slopes arose, — the hills were everywhere.
The eye pent long to narrow walls drank in
The vast horizon, resting gratefully
On awful depths and breadths, and moving lines
Of varied shadow, — purple, brown, and black,
And to the weary ear came soothingly
The silence broken only by the rush
Of the invisible garments of the wind,
That trailed along the tree tops leagues below.

Goodbye rich evenings, when a glorious light
Streamed through the hill-gaps, touching tenderly
The smooth, green fields, and wavy forest lines,
And threw a mantle of deep black and gold
Across the shoulders of the eastern range,
Which darkened, darkened, till the quiet sky
Was sprinkled thick with stars, and in the north
The long Aurora leaped in quivering flames.

"Goodbye sweet days, goodbye, goodbye!" the voice
Is still, and even the tossing echoes cease;
And so we turn to go, and all the forms
Of hill and vale fade from our lingering eye.

Jefferson, N. H., 1885.

HUGH CRESSY, — BENEDICTINE.

My God. I dreamed in quiet paths to walk,
    There thought Thy voice to lead.
Few friends, calm studies, sober-thoughted talk,
    My utmost need.

Dreamed in those sunny cloisters, far away
    Beside the Tuscan sea,
From purer hearts than mine to catch each day
    Some glimpse of Thee.

But in my soul where self-traced words of gold
    Thy hand wrote words of flame:
"Thou hast renounced for visions dim and cold
    Christ's path of shame!

In tourneys gay and gallant courtesies
    Shall true knights waste their might?
Would'st thou misuse in narrow sympathies
    Thy clearer sight?"

Vicisti Galilæe! yet forgive,
    Forgive if faint with strife.
I hope somewhere, somehow, again to live
    That quiet life.

Did I not learn it at my mother's knee,
    "There sin and sorrow cease!"
In heaven is that life selfish which would be
    A life of peace?